eat
your
way
to
health

Recipes for Success

Nadin

Best wishes!

Isim xx + Estelita xx

eat your way to health

Recipes for Success

Issy Warrack
with Estrelita van Rensburg

contents

CHAPTER 1
introduction

This morning I recollected a conversation I had with a very good friend. We were talking about our book, *Eat Well or Die Slowly*, just as we were finalising its publication. Her question was, 'What are you going to do next?' I laughed and thought to myself 'Good question!', as my answer was to have a good rest!

She knows us very well though, and yes, Estrelita and I had already been discussing our next project – this keto/low-carb cookbook. Like so many subjects these days (and food is no different), there are many opinions as to what is healthy and what is not. What should we eat to maintain optimum health? What is a healthy diet? The questions and opinions are endless.

We, however, speak from experience and can comfortably share what has made us feel so healthy. By following the low carb healthy fats (LCHF)/keto principles, I have lost weight, no longer have brain fog, have more energy, am off all high blood pressure medication, and feel 20 years younger – in fact, like a million dollars. So, what changes did I make?

People always want to know, 'What are you doing differently to what you have done before?' When I tell them, their immediate reaction is usually one of the following: It doesn't follow the existing dietary guidelines, it sounds very difficult, it's hard to follow, there's not much variety, we're told not to eat too much dairy, isn't all that fat bad for you? etc., etc.

We have all been brought up to accept the opinions of people in authority, so, for some of us, it goes against the grain (forgive the pun) to challenge authority, especially if it is medical advice and, in this specific case, government nutritional advice.

In our book, *Eat Well or Die Slowly*, we explained the inaccuracies of the national nutritional guidelines – inaccuracies that exist in all the Western world. We then offered guidance on what types of food we should eat – basically the same type of diet that our ancestors ate when lifestyle diseases had not manifested themselves.

Our Healthy Eating Guidelines

The aim of our recipes is to improve your metabolic health and, in so doing, you will experience one or many of the following:

- Reduced sugar addiction
- Improved overall health
- Weight loss
- Enhanced mental focus (less brain fog)
- Improved mood
- Improved physical performance
- Few (if any) food cravings
- Better sleep
- Improved blood glucose levels
- No hunger pangs
- More energy
- Improved blood pressure (lower blood pressure)
- Reduced medication

It all sounds too good to be true, doesn't it? But, if you are interested in any (or all) of the above, read on.

Metabolic Health

Metabolic health refers to a generally healthy condition with normal levels for all biomarkers – e.g. hormones such as insulin and cortisol, and other blood biochemistry markers such as glucose, HbA1c, triglycerides – without the use of medication.

Doesn't that sound good?

Just think what a difference that would make to your life. It certainly made a difference to ours.

So, let's get going!

Net Carbohydrate Count – The Relevance for Keto/LCHF

All our lives we have been told to count calories, calories this and calories that. Nearly every diet says 'reduce your calories, take more exercise and you will lose weight'. We, however, take no account of calories but pay much more attention to the carbohydrate (carb) values of foods and, in particular, the net carb count.

What do we mean by **net carbs?** I was a little confused myself, so let me explain. To calculate the net carb value of foods, we need to take the carbohydrate value then deduct the fibre content. For example, if a food has 10g of carbohydrates and 4g of fibre, the net carb value is 6g.

So, what is the correct or ideal net carb value that one should aim for? We know that our daily net carb intake levels are closely related to our metabolic health. The higher our intake, the more likely we are to develop insulin resistance and, over time, one or more of the lifestyle diseases.

There is not an absolute daily net carb value that will suit every person, but we know from experience that most people who don't carry excess weight nor suffer from lifestyle diseases consume, on average, between 20 and 50g of net carbs daily. For some people, it can be higher – up to 100g or even 150g.

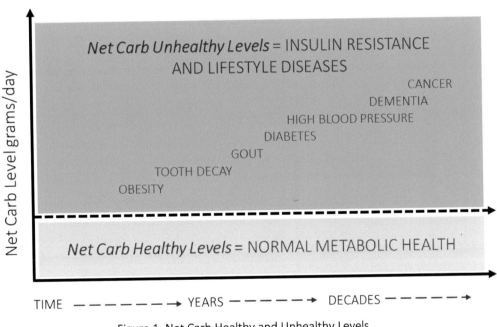

Figure 1. Net Carb Healthy and Unhealthy Levels

We do recommend, however, that if you wish to lose weight or improve your metabolic health (e.g. if you wish to reduce your diabetes medication or even achieve type 2 diabetes remission), that you do not exceed the 20g daily level until you achieve your goal. Once you have achieved your goal, it is important that you maintain a healthy net carb level, to prevent relapsing into a metabolic disease state again.

You may wonder how to determine the correct net carb level for your body. Good question. We suggest that a very good indicator is the number of grams of net carbs you can eat each day whilst neither losing nor gaining weight or if you are taking medication, that this is kept at a constant or reduced level.

It's also helpful to keep track of and record how you respond to certain types of food. You may find that there are some foods you simply cannot handle or must eat in limited amounts to prevent regaining weight and stimulating cravings. In time, you may find that foods made with white flour or other refined grains and starchy foods do not taste as wonderful as you remembered them. This is certainly the case for us!

If you are on a keto low-carb diet (below 20 grams a day), you need to be very careful what you eat. Figure 2 below provides carb value ranges for different types of food. Vegetables in the green area (above-the-ground, green leafy vegetables) is the group to aim for – they are tasty, rich in nutrients and have very low net carb counts.

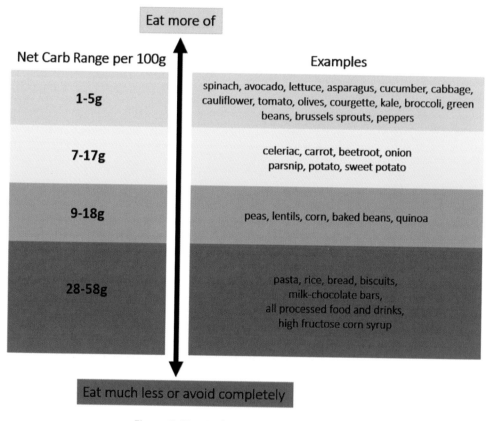

Figure 2. Net Carb Ranges for Food Types

The below-ground vegetables (yellow area) have higher carb values and can be consumed by people on a not-too-strict low-carb diet. The lentil-corn-beans area (orange) is relatively high in carbs and these are not good options for people on a keto low-carb diet. The refined grains and all processed foods and drinks category (red) should be consumed sparingly or avoided. This category has extremely high carb values and will put most people on a fast track to declining metabolic health.

The Importance of Protein and Fats

People who follow a low-calorie intake are often starving – literally! On a low carb programme, starvation is avoided as we eat sufficient amounts of protein and healthy fats which create satiety. You will see these essential components in all of our recipes.

All cells and tissues in our body contain protein; therefore, protein is essential for growth and repair and the maintenance of good health. Since the body does not store excess protein, daily consumption of protein is crucial to keep us strong and healthy.

Healthy fat has very important functions in the body: it forms part of the membrane (protective wall) that surrounds every cell in our body; almost two-thirds of our brain is composed of fat and cholesterol; and our body uses fat as a fuel source, which is a much more efficient fuel source than carbohydrates. Enough fat in our diet ensures that the fat-soluble vitamins (A, D, E and K) are absorbed from the food we eat.

Gluten Sensitivity

Gluten sensitivities are more prevalent now. Years ago, I was diagnosed as being gluten sensitive. In many ways, that appeared to be a blessing as I wasn't able to indulge in cakes and lovely breads. However, there are a variety of gluten-free alternatives on the market and they found their way into my diet. Had I realised how many carbs they contained, and how lacking in real nutrition they were, I might not have been so enamoured.

Real Food: Essential for Metabolic Health

You will notice that we always emphasise the importance of real nutritious food. We eat locally sourced grass-fed meat, free-range eggs, sustainably caught fresh fish (not farmed), vegetables, Jersey full-fat milk, natural yoghurt and delicious full-fat cheese. As mentioned, we definitely do not recommend processed foods due to their high carbohydrate content and the industrialised chemical processes used in their manufacture. Where possible, always cook fresh. Our recipes are designed to be easy to follow and nutritious. Many are ready to eat cooked from scratch in fifteen to thirty minutes.

Focus on quality, not quantity, and champion ethically produced food from local sources.

Artificial Sweeteners

We acknowledge that some people cannot initially accept the taste of unsweetened foods and, in those cases, we do suggest using your favourite sweetener. In time, we find that people so love the taste of the foods in these recipes that they no longer need to use sweeteners. There is research showing that artificial sweeteners are addictive in animals and that people consuming these products daily had a greater risk of developing insulin resistance and type 2 diabetes.

In the herbs and spices section below, you will see that we include cinnamon which can be used as a natural sweetener, so that may be an alternative for you.

Herbs and Spices

One feature of highly processed food is that many different chemical additives are added to enhance their flavour. What better way to add flavour to your food, than growing your own supply of fresh herbs in the garden?

I just love running my fingers through the herbs – somehow it transports me to Provence in France and I can, in an instant, feel the hot sun on my back. Spices, too, are so flavoursome and have the added benefit of being anti-inflammatory. Whilst writing this section, I am reminded of one evening many years ago when an Indian friend came to do a cookery demo for friends. It was a revelation when she brought out the fresh spices – so different from what my taste buds had experienced in Indian restaurants. And that started a lifelong love affair with spices.

Always try to add fresh herbs and spices, both for flavour and for health reasons.

The range of herbs and spices in our recipes include the following:

- Basil – anti-inflammatory.
- Bay Leaves – an excellent source of vitamin A. Use for flavouring.
- Black Pepper, freshly ground – known as the 'King of Spices'.
- Chives – great flavouring.
- Chilli peppers – great for boosting metabolism.
- Cinnamon – natural sweetener as well as anti-inflammatory.
- Coriander – rich in immune-boosting antioxidants.
- Cumin – promotes good digestion.
- Dill – rich in antioxidants.
- Fennel seeds – a powerful antioxidant.
- Garlic – good for heart health.
- Ginger – digestive benefits, anti-inflammatory.
- Nutmeg – both antioxidant and anti-inflammatory properties.
- Oregano – a powerful antioxidant.
- Paprika – nutrient rich.
- Parsley – rich in antioxidants.
- Rosemary – anti-inflammatory.
- Sage – helps with hot flushes, use as an infusion.
- Sea Salt – prevents muscle cramps.
- Tarragon – nutrient rich.
- Thyme – anti-inflammatory, antioxidant.
- Turmeric - anti-inflammatory, antioxidant.

Ingredients in this Book

For your convenience, all meat in the recipes is interchangeable; so, if you prefer, say, lamb to beef, just swap that ingredient in the recipe.

'You are what you eat eats.'

Michael Pollan

Conversion Tables

LIQUID MEASUREMENTS		
Metric (ml)	Imperial (oz)	Cups
30	1	⅛
60	2	¼
80	2½	⅓
125	4	½
150	5	
185	6	¾
250	8½	1
300	10	
375	12½	1½
500	17	2
600	20	2½
750	25	3
1000	34	4
Metric (ml)	Imperial (oz)	Spoons
45	1½	3 tbs

DRY WEIGHT MEASUREMENTS		
Metric (g)	Imperial (oz)	Cups
10	⅓	
30	1	
50	1¾	
100	3½	
250	9	1
500	17½	2
750	26½	3
1000	35⅕	4
Metric (g)	Imperial (oz)	Spoons
5	⅙	1 tsp
15	½	1 tbs

tsp = teaspoon; tbs = tablespoon

TEMPERATURES	
Fahrenheit (°F)	Celsius (°C)
500	260
450	230
400	200
350	175
300	150
250	120

How to use the Cookbook

Throughout the book (unless stated otherwise): **Servings are for 2 persons**.

ITEM	EXPLANATION
carbs	abbreviation for carbohydrates
tbs	tablespoon
tsp	teaspoon
	net carb value in grams – *per serving*
	use hob
	use oven – temperature alongside in degrees Celsius
5 mins	hands-on time to prepare
5 mins/50 mins	time to prepare/total time (which includes fridge time and/or cooking time).

CHAPTER 2

essential alternatives

Vegetable Rice

An appetising and nourishing alternative.

 4-5g   8 min

- 250g cauliflower, or
- 250g broccoli, or
- 250g courgettes
  cut into florets or chunks
- a drizzle of olive oil for cooking
- 1 tbs butter
- sea salt and black pepper

1. *Place vegetable of choice in the food processor; pulse on and off quickly until it forms 'rough grains.'*
2. *Don't overdo it – the key is to preserve the texture of the vegetable and not let it go to mush.*
3. *Drizzle olive oil into a large frying pan, add salt and pepper and spread around the base to prevent vegetables sticking.*
4. *Turn the heat up high.*
5. *Add vegetables and stir briskly for 3 min.*
6. *Add butter, allowing it to melt.*
7. *Serve immediately.*

TIP
Cauliflower will go light brown and has a nutty taste, whilst broccoli rice is softer in consistency. Courgette rice makes smaller grains and is the softest of the three.

Vegetable Zoodles

*Courgettes are an awesome substitute for pasta
when prepared this way.*

 5g   5 min

- 250g courgettes
- 1 tbs olive oil
- 2 cloves garlic, chopped
- sea salt and black pepper
- 2 tbs parmesan cheese, grated

1. *Spiralise the courgettes.*
2. *Pan-fry garlic in olive oil for 1 min.*
3. *Add salt and pepper.*
4. *Add the spiralised courgettes for 1 min maximum (less, if you really like your vegetables al dente).*
5. *Sprinkle parmesan and serve immediately.*

Cauliflower Mash

The healthy flavoursome option to potato mash.

 5g

 8 min

1. *Chop florets into small pieces.*
2. *Pan-fry garlic in 1 tbs butter for 1 min.*
3. *Add salt and pepper, then add 2 or 3 tbs water and cauliflower florets and thyme.*

- 250g head cauliflower
- 3 tbs butter
- 2 cloves garlic, chopped
- 2 sprigs thyme, chopped
- 2 tbs cream
- lemon, zest and juice
- sea salt and black pepper

4. *Steam gently (lid closed) for 3 min.*
5. *Blend cauliflower (if you like fine puree) or mash for a rougher texture.*
6. *Add remaining butter, cream, lemon zest and juice.*
7. *Mix thoroughly.*
8. *Serve immediately.*

Mayonnaise

Absolutely delicious mayonnaise with no sugar –
unlike commercial products!

 0g

 5 min

4 SERVINGS

- 1 egg yolk
- 1 tbs Dijon mustard
- 250ml olive oil
- 2 tsp lemon juice
- sea salt and black pepper

> NOTE: Egg and mustard must be at room temperature, otherwise it will curdle.

1. *Mix egg yolk and mustard in a blender and slowly add olive oil in a thin stream. The mayo should start to thicken.*
2. *Continue to mix until all the oil is added and the mayo set.*
3. *Add lemon juice and season with salt and pepper.*
4. *Taste and adjust seasoning if necessary.*
5. *Store in the fridge.*

Vinaigrette Dressing

Keeps in the fridge for up to 5 days.

 1.5g

 5 min/65 min

4 SERVINGS

- 45ml quality balsamic vinegar
- 1 clove garlic, diced
- ¾ tsp black pepper
- ¾ tsp sea salt
- 1 ½ tsp Dijon mustard
- 75ml olive oil

Mix all ingredients and allow to sit for an hour before using to allow the flavours to meld together.

Mixed Green Vegetables

*A totally innovative way to quickly cook green vegetables,
retaining the flavour and bite.*

 3g   7 min

**SELECT ANY 3 OR 4 OF THE
FOLLOWING VEGGIES:**
- 30g spring greens, chopped
- 30g broccoli, chopped
- 30g cabbage, chopped
- 30g kale, shredded
- 30g green beans, chopped
- 30g runner beans, chopped
- 2 cloves garlic, chopped
- 2 tbs olive oil
- 2 tbs butter
- ½ tsp harissa paste
  (optional)
- sea salt and pepper

1. *Pan-fry the veggies in butter and olive oil, adding salt, pepper and garlic – ensure the veggies are well coated.*
2. *Add 2 tbs water and seal with lid.*
3. *Steam for about 3 min depending on how crispy you like your veg. If using spinach, add for the last minute of steaming.*
4. *Add harissa paste for extra flavour (if using).*
5. *Serve immediately.*

Seed Bread

Normal bread has very high carb values.

If you love bread, make this your healthy option.

MAKES 10 SLICES

 2g   175°C    10 min/55 min

- 55g almond flour
- 3 tbs coconut flour
- 25g sesame seeds
- 2 tbs chia seeds
- 1 tsp poppy seeds
- 1 tbs psyllium powder
- ¾ tsp baking powder
- ¼ tsp salt
- 55g cream cheese
- 2 eggs
- 2 tbs butter
- 3 tbs thick cream

1. Mix the first 8 ingredients in a bowl.
2. Whisk/process cream cheese, eggs, butter and cream.
3. Add to the dry mix.
4. Line a baking tin with greaseproof paper.
5. Add mix to tin.
6. Bake for 45 min.
7. Test if cooked by piercing with a knife. The knife should be clean.
8. Take out of the oven and remove bread from the baking tin.
9. Remove greaseproof paper.
10. Cool loaf on a rack – if left in the tin, the crust will become soggy.

Natural Home-made Yoghurt

Enjoy the quality, texture and taste of your own yoghurt!

 2g    50 min/8h50 min

- 1 litre full-fat milk
- 3 tbs live full-fat natural yoghurt

1. *Pour milk into a pan and heat to 85°C.*
2. *Leave to cool to 46°C.*
3. *Whisk in 3 tbs live yoghurt.*
4. *Pour into a bowl and seal with lid.*
5. *Place in the hot water tank cupboard for 8 hours, or outside the fridge if you live in a warm climate.*
6. *Leave longer for a thicker, creamier version.*
7. *Take out and transfer to another bowl or jars and store in the fridge.*

TIP *There is no need for a yoghurt maker (great if you have one). You will need a pan, thermometer and a bowl with a lid, and an extra bowl or jars to store.*

Soft Homemade Cream Cheese

So much healthier without commercial additives.

 2g/45g (of cream cheese)   25 min

MAKES 250G OF CREAM CHEESE

- 2 litres full-fat milk
- 7 or 8 tbs lemon juice
- sea salt to taste

1. *Pour milk into a pan and bring to boil over medium heat.*
2. *Take the pan off the heat and add lemon juice.*
3. *Set aside for 3 to 5 min whilst milk curdles.*
4. *Curds will form with a yellowish liquid left over.*
5. *After 5 min, all curds should have formed.*
6. *Pour curdled milk through a muslin (cheesecloth) cloth and sieve to strain the liquid.*
7. *Rinse curds with cold water.*
8. *Squeeze the curds to release any extra water.*
9. *Place curds in the blender, add salt and blend for 1 or 2 min until you have a soft texture.*
10. *Keep in the fridge – stores for up to 7 days.*

CHAPTER 3
snacks

Warm Blue Cheese Dip

A perfect healthy snack dish full of essential fats.

 6g   20 min

- 250g natural full-fat yoghurt
- 75g crumbled blue cheese
- 1 tsp basil, chopped
- 1 tsp rosemary, chopped
- 1 tbs chives, finely chopped
- 1 tsp arrowroot to thicken
- 2 tsp black pepper
- 1 tbs parsley, chopped for garnish

1. *Warm the yoghurt in a pan over low heat.*
2. *Add crumbled blue cheese, basil, rosemary and chives, and stir in, moving the mixture around to prevent it sticking to the bottom of the pan.*
3. *Add arrowroot to liquid and stir in.*
4. *Cook gently for 10 min.*
5. *Add pepper.*
6. *Garnish with parsley and serve with cheese chips.*

Cheese Chips

Use your favourite hard cheese.

 0g 200°C 8 min

- 60g grated cheese
- pinch paprika
- thyme/rosemary, chopped

1. *Place mounds of grated cheese onto baking paper on a baking tray.*
2. *Top each round with paprika and herbs.*
3. *Bake for 5 min.*
4. *Allow to cool before serving.*

Dark Chocolate Nut Bars

Absolutely fantastic if you have a sweet tooth!

 0.5g   60 min

- 100g 100% dark chocolate, broken into pieces
- 50g tahini paste
- 2 tbs coconut oil
- 30g macadamia nuts, crushed
- 1 tsp sea salt

1. *Melt the chocolate, tahini paste and coconut oil over very low heat.*
2. *Pour mixture into a tray and place in the fridge for 10 to 15 min until it starts to set.*
3. *Scatter the crushed macadamia nuts and salt on top.*
4. *Lightly press into the chocolate.*
5. *Place back in the fridge and allow to set.*
6. *Cut in 24 pieces using a pizza cutter.*

Protein Balls

 2g   12 min

- 120g nuts (macadamia, walnut, brazil, pecan)
- 90g desiccated coconut
- 40g tahini paste
- 90g coconut oil, melted
- ½ tsp vanilla extract
- 2 tbs water
- ¼ tsp cinnamon
- ¼ tsp sea salt

1. *Grind the nuts in a food processor.*
2. *Add the rest of the ingredients to the processor until a thick paste is formed.*
3. *Make 12 balls and store them in the fridge.*
4. *Can freeze.*

> *NOTE: Initially the balls are soft, but they will harden in the fridge.*

GREAT SNACK FOR ATHLETES ON THE RUN!

Spicy Nuts

Delicious spicy snack described as 'A hint of genius with added bacon!'

 1-2g   150°C 20 min

NUTS HAVE DIFFERENT CARBS:
PECANS 9, WALNUTS 14, ALMONDS 18

- 3 rashers streaky bacon
- 2 tbs butter
- 200g pecans/almonds/walnuts
- 1 tbs coconut oil
- ½ tsp cumin
- ½ tsp chilli powder
- ½ tsp cinnamon
- 1 tbs water
- 1 tbs sea salt

1. *Fry bacon in half the butter, then chop fried bacon into small pieces.*
2. *Keep the fat.*
3. *Toast nuts in a separate large pan until they are golden.*
4. *Add the bacon fat and 1 tbs butter to the pan and cook until nuts darken.*
5. *Add water and bacon pieces and toss everything together.*
6. *Place nuts on a tray in the oven and bake for 5 min.*
7. *Add salt, allow to cool and place in an airtight container.*

Baked Seed Crackers

Serve with dairy butter, cheese, chicken liver pate, or charcuterie.

SERVES 15 SNACKS

 0.5g   150°C    15 min/55 min

- 20g sunflower seeds
- 20g pumpkin seeds
- 20g almond flour
- 25g sesame seeds
- 25g chia seeds
- 20g coconut oil
- ½ tbs psyllium husks
- 100ml water
- 1 tsp sea salt

1. *Mix all dry ingredients in a bowl.*
2. *Add boiling water and coconut oil.*
3. *Mix with a fork and form a dough.*
4. *Take 2 pieces of baking paper, and place the dough between them.*
5. *Roll the dough out thinly with a rolling pin.*
6. *Place the dough on the bottom paper and onto a baking tray and bake for 40 min.*
7. *Check towards the end that they are not burning as seeds are heat sensitive.*
8. *Turn the oven off and leave the dough on the tray to dry.*
9. *When cool, take out and break into pieces.*

TIP

Place surplus in airtight container to keep fresh.
Seeds are interchangeable if you don't have the right ones in your cupboard.

Chicken Liver Pate

SERVES 6

 1g   20 min

- ½ onion
- 1 garlic clove
- 125g butter
- 270g chicken livers
- 1 tbs brandy
- 2 tsp tomato paste
- sea salt and black pepper
- 4 tbs butter, melted

1. *Finely chop garlic and onion.*
2. *Fry in 2 tbs butter.*
3. *Remove and add further 1 tbs butter and fry liver on all sides.*
4. *Add brandy, salt and pepper.*
5. *Lower heat and reduce the juices.*
6. *Allow to cool, then...*
7. *Blend the fried onion, garlic and liver, and mix to a smooth batter with the remainder of the butter and tomato paste.*
8. *Place in dish and cover with the melted butter.*
9. *Chill in the fridge before serving.*
10. *Serve with Seed Crackers.*

LEFT ABOVE: *Warm blue cheese dip with cheese crackers.*
LEFT BELOW: *Chicken liver pate with seed crackers and butter.*

Egg Muffins

 1g   175ºC  10 min/40 min

- eggs (1 egg per 2 servings: make as many as you wish)
- sea salt and black pepper

FILLINGS: CHOOSE ANY OF THE FOLLOWING:

- leftover veg – kale, courgettes, asparagus, spinach, tomato, bell-pepper, mushrooms.
- Chicken/turkey leftovers, fried chopped bacon
- cheese, grated

1. *Whisk eggs, salt and pepper.*
2. *Grease a muffin/cupcake tin and divide mixture into however many you are making.*
3. *Fill ½ full and sprinkle on your chosen fillings.*
4. *Bake for up to 30 min until cooked and golden.*
5. *Cool.*
6. *Store in the fridge or freeze.*

Smoked Mackerel Pate

SERVES 3 TO 4

 1.5g   5 min

- 2 smoked mackerel fillets (or other smoked fish)
- 3 spring onions or ½ medium onion, chopped
- 1 clove garlic, chopped
- 30g cream cheese
- 30g crème fraiche
- 1 tsp horseradish sauce
- sprig parsley or 1 tsp dried parsley
- ½ tsp chilli powder
- lemon juice
- sea salt and black pepper

1. *Remove skin from fish fillets and check for bones.*
2. *Flake the fish in a bowl and mix with all the ingredients.*
3. *Fork until obtaining the consistency you wish (process for a finer consistency).*
4. *Serve with seed crackers.*

morning kick starters

Healthy Way of Life

Health Check

Well

User

ht Loss an

simple – an easy-t

Bullet Coffee

A great way to start the day!

 0g   5 min

- 1 cup filter coffee
- 1 tbs butter or ghee
- 1 tbs coconut oil
- 1 or 2 tbs cream (optional)
- pinch cinnamon (optional)

1. *Process all ingredients or blend with a stick blender.*
2. *Serve immediately.*
3. *If serving with cream, pour on top.*
4. *If serving with cinnamon, sprinkle on top.*

Smoothies: Berries or Healthy Green

 8g

 5g

- 75g strawberries or raspberries
- splash lemon juice or orange zest
- splash vanilla extract
- pinch of cinnamon
- 1 tbs coconut oil
- 100g natural full-fat yoghurt

- 100g full-fat natural yoghurt
- ½ avocado
- large handful spinach
- 1 tbs coconut oil or olive oil.
- add water if you prefer a lighter consistency.

USE A BLENDER TO LIQUIDISE ALL INGREDIENTS AND ENJOY!

SUBSTITUTE YOGURT WITH COCONUT CREAM/MILK OR FULL-FAT MILK.

EASY-PEASY

Berries and Yogurt

Add together: 100g of yogurt, 75g of raspberries or strawberries and top with almonds.

 8g

GREAT FOR BREAKFAST, BRUNCH, LUNCH OR DESSERT.

Porridge with Chia & Sesame Seeds

 8g   5 min

- 1 tbs chia seeds
- 1 tbs sesame seeds
- 1 egg
- 5 tbs cream
- pinch salt
- 30g butter
- 75g berries

1. *Mix all ingredients except for the fruit and butter.*
2. *Cook in the butter.*
3. *Serve with fruit.*

Granola

5 SERVINGS

 2.5g   150°C    15 min/55 min

- 50g pecans or hazelnuts
- 20g shredded coconut
- 35g sunflower seeds
- 8g pumpkin seeds
- 10g sesame seeds
- 35g flaxseed
- ¼ tsp turmeric
- ¼ tsp cinnamon
- ½ tsp vanilla extract
- 15g almond flour
- 60ml filtered water
- 15ml coconut oil, melted

1. *Chop nuts, and add all ingredients.*
2. *Mix.*
3. *Place in the oven for 20 min.*
4. *Stir.*
5. *Leave for further 20 min.*
6. *Serve with natural full-fat yoghurt.*

Chapter 4 morning kick starters

Bacon, Egg, Avocado and Tomato Salad

For variety, use smoked salmon or mackerel instead of bacon.

 5g   5 min

- 1 ripe avocado
- 2 boiled eggs
- 1 large tomato
- lemon juice
- 4 slices cooked bacon
- 3 tbs sour cream
- sea salt and black pepper

1. *Chop all ingredients.*
2. *Add lemon juice and top with sour cream.*
3. *Cook bacon then crumble into pieces and serve on top.*
4. *Season with salt and pepper.*

QUICK IDEA
Scrambled Eggs

Chop some halloumi, bacon and onion.
Fry in olive oil.
Add one or two whisked eggs, lower heat and cook for 1-2 min.
Top with olives and chives. Serve with a fresh salad.

Chapter 4 morning kick starters

Spinach, Goat's Cheese and Chorizo Omelette

 5g   12 min

- 100g chorizo, sliced
- 1 tbs butter
- 3 eggs
- 1 tbs water
- a handful of spinach leaves
- 50g crumbled goat's cheese
- sliced avocado

1. *Fry chorizo for 3 min in butter, take out and put aside.*
2. *Beat eggs, add eggs to pan, then add chorizo, spinach and goat's cheese on half of the egg mixture.*
3. *Cook on low heat for 3 min until slightly firm, then fold over.*
4. *Leave for few min until eggs are cooked through.*
5. *Serve with sliced avocado.*

> **TIP**
> *Replace chorizo with fried bell-peppers or mushrooms.*
> *Replace goat's cheese with fried halloumi or mozzarella cheese.*

'Don't eat anything that your great-great-grandmother wouldn't recognise as food.'

Michael Pollan

Poshrooms

Simple to make and ready in minutes!

 7g

 10 min

- 150g chanterelle mushrooms, sliced
- 2 cloves garlic, chopped
- 2 tbs full-fat butter
- a handful of fresh herbs – thyme, oregano, rosemary, chopped
- 2 slices seed bread
- 100g ricotta cheese
- 30g parmesan, grated

1. *Slice and fry mushrooms and garlic in butter with half of the chopped herbs.*
2. *Toast seed bread and cover with full-fat butter.*
3. *Spread ricotta over buttered toast.*
4. *Cover with fried mushrooms.*
5. *Sprinkle with parmesan and more fresh herbs.*

CHAPTER 5
salads

Salad Toppings

Healthy and quick ideas to add bite to your salads.

 1g

- sesame seeds
- pumpkin seeds
- sunflower seeds
- pecan, chopped
- walnuts, chopped
- coconut, shredded
- almonds, chopped,
- macadamia nuts, chopped

Make a crunchy topping with a teaspoon of 3 of the seeds or make a mixture of your favourites and store in an airtight container.

Celery and Iceberg Salad with Vinaigrette Dressing

Sharp tangy salad, perfect for serving with cold salmon.

 1g   10 min

- ½ lemon, juiced
- 1 tsp Dijon mustard
- I shallot, chopped
- 2 tbs olive oil
- 50g halloumi, sliced
- 4 iceberg lettuce wedges
- 1 celery stalk, sliced
- 2 sprigs parsley or dill
- sea salt and black pepper

1. *Combine lemon juice, mustard, shallot and 1 tbs olive oil in a bowl for dressing.*
2. *Season with salt and pepper.*
3. *Pan-fry halloumi in 1 tbs olive oil, then slice into small pieces.*
4. *Arrange wedges of lettuce on a plate.*
5. *Scatter celery, halloumi and sprigs of parsley/dill over the lettuce.*
6. *Drizzle with dressing.*
7. *Serve immediately.*

Dreamy Cucumber Salad

A delicious accompaniment to Cape Malay Curry.

 2g 10 min/1h10 min

- 60ml thick cream
- ½ lemon, juiced
- 2 tbs parsley, chopped
- ⅓ cucumber, chopped
- 1 shallot, sliced
- sea salt and black pepper

1. *Mix the cream, lemon juice and parsley in a bowl.*
2. *Add cucumber and shallot.*
3. *Mix well.*
4. *Cover and place in the fridge for 60 min.*
5. *Season with salt and pepper and mix through again.*
6. *Serve immediately.*

Red Bell-Pepper and Anchovy Salad

 3g 220°C 30 min

- 2 large bell-peppers
- 2 tbs olive oil
- 2 eggs, hardboiled
- handful parsley, chopped
- 2 garlic cloves, chopped
- 2 tbs olive oil
- 8 anchovy fillets
- basil, a small handful
- salt and pepper

1. *Cut the peppers in half, place on a baking tray and drizzle with olive oil.*
2. *Bake for 20 min.*
3. *Boil eggs and then cut in half.*
4. *Slice pepper flesh into strips.*
5. *Mix parsley and garlic with more olive oil and season with salt and pepper.*
6. *Place pepper strips on a plate; top with parsley/garlic dressing.*
7. *Then place halved eggs on top of the dressing.*
8. *Add 2 anchovy fillets over each egg half.*
9. *Top with basil leaves.*
10. *Serve immediately.*

Tossed Salad with Pan-fried Beef Strips

Ideal for a satisfying summer's day lunch or dinner.

4g 20 min

- 250g rump steak
- 2 tbs butter
- lettuce, 2 handfuls of leaves
- nasturtium flowers
- 50g broccoli, chopped
- 50g asparagus, chopped
- 2 tbs olive oil
- 1 piece cooked beetroot
- 2 vine tomatoes
- chicory leaves
- pine nuts
- sesame seeds
- 50g blue cheese

1. *Pan-fry steak in butter.*
2. *Allow to cool slightly, then cut into strips.*
3. *Wash lettuce and nasturtium flowers and leaves.*
4. *Fry broccoli and asparagus in olive oil seasoned with salt and pepper for 1 or 2 min.*
5. *Add 1 tbs water and steam for 2 min.*
6. *Chop beetroot.*
7. *Quarter tomatoes.*
8. *Chop chicory leaves.*
9. *Dry fry the sesame seeds and pine nuts. Take care not to burn.*
10. *Dice blue cheese.*
11. *Arrange the contents of the salad bowl starting with lettuce and nasturtium flowers, add the cooked veg, beetroot, tomatoes and chicory leaves.*
12. *Toss the nuts and seeds over the salad.*
13. *Place meat strips over the top of the salad.*
14. *Toss blue cheese cubes on top.*
15. *Serve with vinaigrette dressing.*

versatile eggs

Baked Eggs

 2.5g   200°C  10 min/20 min

- 2 tbs olive oil
- 4 slices bacon, diced
- 2 cloves garlic, chopped
- ½ red chilli or ½ tsp chilli powder
- 8 cherry tomatoes, chopped
- Sea salt and black pepper
- 2 large eggs
- 50g parmesan, grated
- 1 tbs chopped fresh coriander or parsley

1. *Fry the bacon and garlic in olive oil over medium heat.*
2. *Add chilli and tomatoes, fry for 5 min until tomatoes are cooked through.*
3. *Season with salt and pepper.*
4. *When cooked, spread mixture evenly in individual ovenproof dishes.*
5. *Make a hole in the mixture and crack one egg into each dish; sprinkle with parmesan and parsley.*
6. *Bake for 5–10 min until the egg is cooked to your liking.*

Frittata with Fresh Chard

A glorious-tasting, rich, nutritious dish.

 5g   175°C  15 min/40 min

- 70g bacon, diced
- 50g mushrooms, diced
- 4 tbsp butter
- 2 cloves garlic, sliced
- ¼ chilli, chopped
- 100g Swiss chard
- 4 eggs
- 100ml double cream
- 70g mozzarella cheese
- sea salt and black pepper

1. *Grease a small baking dish.*
2. *Fry bacon, mushrooms, garlic, chilli and chard stalks in butter on medium heat, until cooked.*
3. *Then add chopped chard leaves and 1 tbs water, cover and steam for 2 min.*
4. *Whisk eggs and cream and pour into baking dish.*
5. *Place bacon mixture on top of the egg mix.*
6. *Top with mozzarella and season with salt and pepper.*
7. *Bake for 25 min.*
8. *Served with a fresh green salad, dressed with extra virgin olive oil.*

Simple Welsh Rarebit

Such a simple, mouth-watering meal in minutes.

 4g   15 min

- 150g spinach
- 1 tbs olive oil
- 75g bacon or Parma ham, diced (optional)
- 2 slices seed bread
- 2 tbs full-fat butter
- 2 tsp Dijon mustard
- 2 eggs, poached
- 50g parmesan, grated

1. Lightly fry spinach in olive oil, then add 1 tbs water, cover and steam lightly for 2 min. Drain if necessary.
2. Fry bacon or use Parma ham instead.
3. Toast bread and spread with butter, then mustard.
4. Poach eggs.
5. Place cooked spinach on buttered toast, top with bacon (or ham) and then add a poached egg on top and sprinkle with parmesan.
6. Serve immediately.

Baked Avocado Eggs

 3g 200°C ⏱ 5 min/20 min

- avocado
- 50g salami
- 4 cherry tomatoes
- 1 tbs basil or oregano
- 2 eggs
- 50g mozzarella, shredded
- 2 tbs parsley, chopped
- sea salt and black pepper

1. Halve the avocado and remove the stone, scoop out a little flesh to create space for the egg.
2. Dice salami.
3. Halve cherry tomatoes.
4. Chop basil (or oregano).
5. Crack eggs and add to each hollowed-out avocado, sprinkle with diced salami and surround with tomatoes and chopped basil.
6. Bake for 10 min, then add shredded mozzarella, salt and pepper and bake for further 5 min.
7. Serve immediately.
8. Garnish with chopped parsley.

Chapter 6 versatile eggs

Tarte Flambee

The combination of bacon and Gruyere cheese is just heavenly.

6g 210°C 10 min/35 min

CRUST
- 3 eggs
- 150g mozzarella
- 1 tbs butter

TOPPING
- 1 tbs olive oil
- 1 shallot, thinly sliced
- 2 cloves garlic, thinly sliced
- 80g streaky bacon, chopped
- 125g full fat crème fraiche
- 125g Gruyere or Emmental cheese, grated
- nutmeg, grated
- sea salt and black pepper
- green salad

1. *Make the low-carb dough by mixing together the eggs and mozzarella.*
2. *Line a baking tray with grease proof paper (grease with butter if preferred).*
3. *Place the dough on the grease proof paper and form into a rectangular shape.*
4. *Bake for 15 min and remove from oven.*
5. *For the topping, fry shallot, garlic and bacon in olive oil until the fat is golden brown.*
6. *Dry on kitchen paper.*
7. *Spread the dough with crème fraiche. Scatter the bacon mix over the dough and scatter grated cheese over.*
8. *Season with salt and pepper and some grated nutmeg.*
9. *Bake for further 10 min until base crisp.*
10. *Cut into portions with a pizza cutter.*
11. *Serve immediately with salad.*

> **TIP**
> *The simple low-carb crust can be used as a base for any savoury tart, including pizza!*

LEFT: *Torridon, Scotland*

CHAPTER 7

vegetables
and cheese

Vegetable Soup

Serve with cheese chips or crackers.

 9g   25 min

- 1 shallot, chopped
- 150g broccoli, chopped
- 250ml filtered water
- 1 stock cube
- 100g cream cheese
- 100ml cream or coconut cream milk
- 60g fresh herbs
- 1 clove garlic, chopped
- sea salt and black pepper

1. *Throw all ingredients in a pot and cook for 20 min.*
2. *Liquidise for a creamy smooth texture.*

> **TIP**
>
> *Instead of broccoli, use whichever vegetables you have in the fridge.*

Roast Aubergine with Chilli and Mint Dressing

 8g   200°C  10 min/50 min

- 2 medium aubergines
- 6 tbs olive oil
- 200g spinach
- 1 garlic clove, chopped
- 1 tbs tahini
- 1 tsp lemon juice
- a handful of parsley, chopped, for garnish
- sea salt and black pepper
- buttered slice of seed bread for serving

DRESSING
- ½ red chilli, chopped
- 5 mint leaves, finely chopped
- 1 spring onion, chopped
- 2 tbs balsamic vinegar

1. Cut the aubergines in half.
2. Place skin side down on a baking tray and cover with 2 tbs of olive oil.
3. Bake for 40 min until tender.
4. Make the dressing by mixing all ingredients in a bowl. Set aside.
5. Add I tbs olive oil to a pan, add salt and pepper, toss spinach in the pan, add 1 tbs water and steam for 1 min. Set aside.
6. Using a stick blender, blend garlic, tahini, lemon juice and 3 tbs olive oil.
7. Remove the aubergine from the oven and scoop out the flesh from one aubergine (two halves).
8. Add aubergine flesh to tahini mix and blend again.
9. Season with salt and pepper.
10. Place a remaining aubergine halves on each plate (one half on each plate).
11. Spoon tahini/aubergine mix over each one and top with chilli dressing.
12. Garnish with parsley and serve with buttered seed bread.

Herby Halloumi served on Spicy Kale with Yoghurt Dressing

A heavenly herby dish with a tangy sauce.

 5g   150°C    15 min/30 min

- 125g halloumi, sliced
- handful herbs, chopped
- 3 tbs olive oil
- 100g kale
- ½ tsp chilli
- 2 eggs
- 1 tsp Dijon mustard
- 75g full-fat yoghurt
- 1 tsp white wine vinegar
- avocado
- sea salt and black pepper

1. *Fry halloumi in 2 tbs olive oil with half the handful of chopped herbs and set aside.*
2. *Wash and dry kale.*
3. *Place in an ovenproof dish.*
4. *Add 1 tbs olive oil and mix into kale; sprinkle with ½ tsp chilli powder and season with salt and pepper.*
5. *Bake in the oven for 15 min.*
6. *Poach the 2 eggs.*
7. *Whisk mustard with yoghurt; add salt and pepper and white wine vinegar.*
8. *Slice the avocado.*
9. *Place a handful of kale on plate, place slices of fried halloumi on top, add sliced avocado and smother with yoghurt dressing.*
10. *Top with poached egg and remaining herbs.*

Chapter 7 vegetables and cheese

Quick Mixed Veg Roast topped with Mozzarella

Easy to prepare – can even be prepared in the morning and popped in the oven when you are finished work!

 9g 175°C  10 min/35 min

- 120g bell-pepper, chopped
- 90g kale leaves, chopped
- 25g mushrooms, chopped
- ½ medium red onion, chopped
- 2 garlic cloves, chopped
- 40g asparagus spears
- 130g chicory leaves
- Sea salt and black pepper
- 4 or 5 tbs olive oil
- ¼ tsp red chilli powder
- 100g mozzarella, grated

1. Add all ingredients (apart from grated cheese) to an ovenproof dish.
2. Bake for 15 min.
3. Take out and add mozzarella.
4. Bake for further 10 min until cheese is melted.
5. Serve immediately.

Brussels Sprouts with Delicious Bacon

 6g

 15 min

- 3 rashers bacon
- 1 tbs butter
- 1 tbs olive oil
- ½ tsp paprika
- 200g Brussel sprouts, quartered
- 2 cloves garlic, chopped
- 1 tbs water
- salt and pepper

1. *Chop bacon and fry in butter until crispy, then drain on a paper towel.*
2. *Add olive oil, paprika, sprouts, garlic, salt and pepper to the pan.*
3. *Fry on high heat initially, then lower heat.*
4. *Add 1 tbs water and steam for 2 to 3 min.*
5. *Add bacon back into the pan, turn up the heat and fry for 1 min.*
   ADD MORE OLIVE OIL IF NECESSARY.
6. *Serve immediately.*

Creamed Cabbage with Bacon and Mushrooms

The perfect accompaniment for all game dishes.

 2.5g   10 min

- 2 tbs olive oil
- 1 shallot, diced
- 100g shredded cabbage
- 2 rashers streaky bacon, diced
- 1 large mushroom, sliced
- 1 tsp balsamic vinegar
- 20g cream

1. *Heat olive oil in a pan and fry the shallot until cooked.*
2. *Add shredded cabbage and bacon to the pan and cook until the bacon is browned and the cabbage has wilted.*
3. *Add the mushroom and balsamic vinegar.*
4. *Stir for 1 min.*
5. *Add cream and salt and pepper.*
6. *Serve immediately.*

Red Cabbage

 5g   50 min

- ½ red onion, sliced
- 2 cloves garlic, sliced,
- 1 tbs butter
- 250g red cabbage, shredded
- 30ml cider vinegar
- 2 tsp balsamic vinegar
- sea salt and black pepper

1. *Add butter to a pan and fry onion and garlic for 2 to 3 min.*
2. *Add all other ingredients and stir for a few min.*
3. *Cook for 45 min on low heat until cabbage is tender.*
4. *Check a few times to see there is enough moisture and the cabbage doesn't stick to the pan.*
5. *If you prefer, add a little red wine.*

Oven-baked Camembert

 3g 200°C  5 min/15 min

- 1 whole Camembert
- 30g pecans, chopped
- 1 clove garlic, chopped
- 1 tsp rosemary, chopped
- 1 tsp thyme, chopped
- 2 tbs olive oil
- sea salt and black pepper
- 1 tbs parsley, chopped for garnish
- lettuce, tomato and cucumber

1. *Mix nuts, garlic, herbs, olive oil, salt and pepper.*
2. *Spread mixture on top of Camembert.*
3. *Bake for 10 min.*
4. *Serve with parsley as a garnish and a crunchy salad.*

ABOVE: *Loch Drunkie, Trossachs*

CHAPTER 8
fish
and shellfish

Garlic and Parmesan Trout

Trout is an excellent source of protein and omega 3.

 4.5g   180°C  10 min/25 min

- 2 trout fillets
- 2 tbs butter
- 2 cloves garlic, chopped
- 120g Parmesan cheese, grated
- 25g crème fraiche
- 1 tbs chia seeds
- 1 tbs fresh parsley, chopped
- 1 lemon, quartered
- salt and pepper

1. *Prepare an ovenproof dish and grease with butter.*
2. *Place the trout in the dish.*
3. *Season with salt and pepper.*
4. *In a fresh pan, melt the butter and fry garlic.*
5. *Reduce heat and add parmesan, crème fraiche, chia seeds and parsley.*
6. *Pour mixture over trout and bake in the oven for 15 min.*
7. *Serve with lemon quarters and sautéed green beans.*

Chilli Salmon with Asparagus

 2.5g   15 min

- 250g salmon fillets
- 1 tsp red chilli
- 2 tbs olive oil
- 3 tbs butter
- 150g asparagus
- 6 cherry tomatoes, halved
- 1 tbs pine nuts, chopped
- 1 tbs fresh thyme, chopped
- 2 sprigs parsley
- sea salt and black pepper

1. *Mix the chilli with 1 tbs olive oil and brush over salmon.*
2. *Season with salt and pepper.*
3. *Fry the fish in butter for 4 min each side.*
4. *Add asparagus and tomatoes to the fish pan and cook for 2 min.*
5. *Serve the fish on a bed of the asparagus/tomato mixture.*
6. *Garnish with nuts, thyme and sprigs of parsley.*

Moules Frites

With an innovative alternative to potato fries.

 4g   18 min

- 2 tbs butter
- 1 shallot, sliced
- 40g streaky bacon, diced
- 1 sprig fresh thyme
- 100ml dry white wine
- 100ml fish stock
- 500g mussels (if buying fresh, you need to scrub and debeard them) THROW AWAY ANY WITH BROKEN SHELLS
- 100g cream
- splash of lemon juice.
- a handful of parsley, chopped
- sea salt and black pepper

1. *Melt the butter in a large saucepan. Fry the shallot and bacon.*
2. *Add thyme and white wine and cook on high heat for 2 or 3 min.*
3. *Add stock and bring to boil.*
4. *Add mussels to the pan and cover with the lid. Steam for 5 min until mussels open (discarding any that remain closed).*
5. *With a slotted spoon, remove mussels and set aside.*
6. *Add cream to the pan and whisk in.*
7. *Season with lemon juice, half the parsley and salt and pepper.*
8. *Place the mussels back in the pan and stir through so the sauce covers all the shells.*
9. *Serve immediately in bowls with added parsley on top.*

Turnip Fries

Wash and cut ½ turnip (260g) into chip-sized spears (½ cm wide). Place spears in kitchen paper to draw out any excess water; then mix the olive oil, chilli powder, salt and pepper in a bowl.

Pour oil mixture over chips, ensuring they are all coated. Place on a baking tray in the oven for 10 min, then turn and bake for a further 10 min.

Remove from the oven, sprinkle with sea salt and serve immediately.

 5g/130g 200°C 25 min

Lazy Tuna Casserole

 2g 200°C  10 min/25 min

- 2 cans (112g) tuna in water, drained
- 80g crème fraiche
- 1 tbs Dijon mustard
- 125g Gruyere or Emmental cheese
- 1 red onion, chopped
- ¼ tsp chilli powder
- 2 sprigs parsley for garnish
- sea salt and black pepper

1. *Mix tuna, crème fraiche, mustard, half the cheese, onion, salt, pepper and chilli.*
2. *Place mix in ovenproof dish and cover with remaining cheese.*
3. *Bake for 15 min.*
4. *Serve immediately with parsley garnish and a mixed salad.*

Scrumptious Creamy Fish Casserole

Use any white firm fish or even salmon.

 6g   180°C  10 min/30 min

- 1 tbs olive oil
- 150g broccoli, florets and stems
- 1 shallot, chopped
- 2 tsp capers, chopped
- 250g white fish, in pieces
- 2 tbs butter
- 100g baby spinach
- 120g thick cream
- 1 tsp Dijon mustard
- 1 tbs fresh parsley, chopped
- sea salt and black pepper

1. *Chop the broccoli, both florets and stems.*
2. *Fry broccoli in olive oil for 2 min.*
3. *Season with salt and pepper.*
4. *Add shallot and capers and fry for further 1 min.*
5. *Place veg mix in ovenproof dish and place fish on top.*
6. *Top with butter.*
7. *Add baby spinach on top.*
8. *Mix cream, mustard and parsley and place over the spinach.*
9. *Bake for 20 min in oven.*
10. *Serve immediately.*

LEFT: *RRS Discovery, Dundee*

Italian Buttered Prawns in Tomato Garlic Sauce

 4.5g   20 min

- 1 tbs extra virgin olive oil
- 300g prawns
- salt and pepper
- 2 tbs butter
- 2 cloves garlic, sliced
- 125g tomatoes, chopped
- 1 tbs fresh oregano
- 75g spinach
- 50ml double cream
- 25g parmesan
- bunch basil leaves, chopped
- lemon – for garnish
- basil leaves – for garnish

1. *Heat olive oil in a pan and add seasoned prawns.*
2. *Cook through – at least 2 min each side.*
3. *Remove and set aside.*
4. *Reduce heat and add butter.*
5. *Stir in garlic and cook for 1 min.*
6. *Add chopped tomatoes and oregano and season with salt and pepper.*
7. *Cook for 5 min then add spinach and cook for further 1 or 2 min until spinach wilted.*
8. *Stir in the double cream, parmesan and basil.*
9. *Return prawns to pan and stir them. Cook until prawns are heated through.*
10. *Garnish with more basil and lemon wedges.*
11. *Serve immediately.*

QUICK IDEA

Squid and Scallop Stir Fry

Use 125g each of squid (cut in rings) and scallops and mix in a bowl with ½ tsp
chilli powder, 1 tbs tomato paste, 2 cloves garlic (sliced), ½ lemon (juiced),
a pinch of oregano and basil. Marinade for 10 min.
Then heat 2 tbs of butter in a wok and add the seafood mixture.
Stir-fry for up to 8 min until cooked.
SERVE WITH VEGETABLE RICE OR GREEN SALAD.

Delicious Scallops and Bacon in Butter Sauce

0g   15 min

- 4 rashers bacon
- 2 tbs olive oil
- 4 large or 6 medium scallops
- salt and pepper
- 2 tbs lemon juice
- splash or two of white wine
- 1 tbs butter
- 1 tbs fresh parsley, chopped

1. Fry bacon in 1 tbs olive oil.
2. Remove from pan.
3. Dry scallops with a paper towel. Season with salt and pepper.
4. Add 1 tbs olive oil and fry scallops on high heat for up to 4 min each side.
5. Remove from pan.
6. Add lemon juice and wine to pan and scrape butter/oil mixture from the bottom of the pan.
7. Add butter to create a creamy mixture. Add bacon and scallops.
8. Serve with fresh parsley.

Herring Served in Creamy Mustard Sauce

4.5g   15 min

- 2 tbs butter
- 250g herring fillets
- 2 garlic cloves, chopped
- 100ml cream
- 1 tbs Dijon mustard
- parsley, chopped
- 2 tbs extra virgin olive oil
- 50g chanterelle mushrooms
- 50g broccoli, chopped
- 50g chard, chopped
- 50g spinach leaves
- salt and pepper
- parsley, for garnish

1. Pan-fry herring and garlic in butter for a few min.
2. Mix cream, mustard and parsley into the pan with the herring and cook for 2 or 3 min.
3. In a separate pan, fry mushrooms in olive oil then add the rest of the veggies, coating them in this oil.
4. Add 1 tbs of water, close lid and steam for 2 min.
5. Place herring and sauce on a plate and surround with vegetables.
6. Garnish with parsley.

Creamy Hake with Chunky Ratatouille

Find local fresh fish – you can use cod, monkfish or salmon.

 8.5g   30 min

- 1 tbs olive oil
- 1 med aubergine, in chunks
- 3 cloves garlic, chopped
- 2 courgettes, in chunks
- ½ bell-pepper, in chunks
- 2 tomatoes
- a handful of mixed fresh herbs, chopped
- 100ml vegetable stock
- sea salt and black pepper
- 55g cream cheese
- 20g cream
- 2 cloves garlic, chopped
- 250g hake
- 2 tbs butter
- splash of lemon juice
- 20g pine nuts
- 2 basil leaves, chopped

FOR RATATOUILLE
1. *Fry aubergine in olive oil for 5 min.*
2. *Add garlic, cook for 2 min.*
3. *Add courgettes, pepper, tomatoes and chopped herbs.*
4. *Add vegetable stock and season with salt and pepper.*
5. *Cook for 10 min.*

FOR FISH
6. *Mix cream cheese, cream and garlic.*
7. *Fry fish in butter.*
8. *Add a splash of lemon juice.*
9. *Add the cream mixture to the pan.*
10. *Cook until ready.*
11. *Serve fish on a bed of ratatouille, covering the fish with creamy sauce; garnish with pine nuts and basil.*

ABOVE: *River Tiber, Rome*

CHAPTER 9
chicken
and game birds

Cape Malay Curry

A slightly sweet and mild dish. If you prefer hotter, add ½ a red chilli.

 7g   30 min

- 3 tbs olive oil
- ½ onion, chopped
- 2 cloves garlic, chopped
- ¾ inch fresh ginger, finely chopped
- ½ red chilli
- ½ tsp cumin powder
- ½ tsp coriander
- ½ tsp cinnamon
- ½ inch turmeric root, finely sliced
- 2 chicken breasts, diced
- 200ml can coconut cream
- salt and pepper
- a handful of fresh coriander for garnish
- vegetable rice

1. *In a deep-frying pan, fry onion in olive oil until soft.*
2. *Add garlic and ginger and fry for 30 seconds, then add cumin, coriander, cinnamon and turmeric and stir for a further 30 seconds.*
3. *Add chicken and fry for 5 min, until brown.*
4. *Add coconut cream and bring to a simmer. Stir.*
5. *Cover with lid and simmer for 10 min.*
6. *Prepare vegetable rice or zoodles.*
7. *Remove chicken from heat and season with salt and pepper.*
8. *Place a portion of vegetable rice on a plate and add the chicken curry on top of the rice.*
9. *Garnish with fresh coriander.*
10. *Serve immediately.*

> **TIP**
>
> *Can also be cooked with any white fish.*

ABOVE: *District Six, Cape Town*

Chapter 9 chicken and game birds

Chicken and Bean Sprouts Stir Fry

A touch of Chinese.

 5g   15 min

- 1 tbs sesame oil
- 1 tbs olive oil
- 2 tsp ground ginger
- 2 chicken breasts, diced
- ½ bell pepper, red or yellow
- 4 spring onions, sliced
- 2 cloves garlic, sliced
- 1 or 2 tbs soy sauce
- ¼ tsp chilli powder
- 75g bean sprouts
- 75g courgettes, spiralised
- 2 tbs sesame seeds
- parsley, chopped
- sea salt and black pepper

1. *Heat sesame and olive oil in a wok.*
2. *Add ginger and chicken.*
3. *Cook for 5 min then remove from wok.*
4. *Add pepper, onions and garlic and gently cook.*
5. *Add chicken back in and cook through.*
6. *Reduce heat and add soy sauce, chilli powder, bean sprouts and spiralised courgettes.*
7. *Continue to sauté until bean sprouts are wilted.*
8. *Sprinkle sesame seeds and garnish with parsley*
9. *Serve immediately. Enjoy!*

Stuffed Chicken Breasts

With mushrooms and French Comte cheese.

3g 180°C 20 min/50 min

- 2 tbs butter
- 2 tbs olive oil
- 60g mushrooms, chopped
- 2 cloves garlic, chopped
- 25g cream cheese
- 25g Comte cheese, grated
- 1 tbs parsley, chopped
- 1 tsp thyme, chopped
- 2 chicken breasts (preferably skins on)
- glug of white wine
- 50ml chicken stock
- 1 tsp arrowroot, mixed with 1 tbs water
- sea salt and black pepper

1. *Heat 1 tbs butter and 1 tbs olive oil in a pan. Add mushrooms and garlic and fry for 5 min. Season with salt and pepper.*
2. *Remove from heat.*
3. *Mix cream cheese, Comte cheese, parsley and thyme in a bowl.*
4. *Add mushrooms and garlic to bowl and mix thoroughly. Add extra seasoning if required.*
5. *Place mixture under the skin of the chicken breast or, if no skin, create a pocket in the breast.*
6. *In an ovenproof pan, add remaining butter and olive oil and brown the chicken breasts.*
7. *Add a glug of wine.*
8. *Place chicken in oven and cook for 30 min.*
9. *Check chicken; if cooked, its juices should run clear.*
10. *Remove chicken and add the stock with arrowroot to thicken. Scrape all the sides of the dish to pull in the extra flavour.*
11. *Serve with mixed green vegetables.*

'How can you govern a country which has 246 varieties of cheese?'

President Charles de Gaulle

Chapter 9 chicken and game birds

Creamy Peri Peri Chicken Livers with Herbs and Toast

 6g   20 min

- 1 small onion, sliced
- 2 cloves garlic, sliced
- 150g chicken livers, chopped
- 1 tsp fresh thyme, chopped
- 1 tsp rosemary, chopped
- ½ red chilli, finely chopped
- 2 tbs olive oil
- 1 tsp balsamic vinegar
- 100ml double cream
- 1 tbs olive oil
- 150g fresh spinach
- 2 tbs butter
- 2 slices seed bread
- 2 sprigs thyme

1. *Finely slice onion and garlic.*
2. *Mix with chopped chicken livers, chopped thyme, rosemary and red chilli.*
3. *Fry in olive oil on high heat for about 4 min.*
4. *Lower heat and add the balsamic vinegar.*
5. *Add cream and cook for a further 5 min.*
6. *Fry spinach in olive oil, then add a little water and steam for 2 min.*
7. *Toast bread and spread with butter.*
8. *Serve livers on a bed of spinach.*
9. *Serve with buttered toast and garnish with thyme.*

Country Cottage Pie

Can use duck, chicken or minced lamb.

 11g   190°C  25 min/50 min

- ½ fresh red chilli, chopped
- 2 tsp black pepper, ground
- 1 tsp salt
- 250g duck breasts
- 2 tbs butter
- 1 + ½ shallot, chopped
- 1 carrot, chopped
- large pinch of fresh thyme leaves
- 60ml red wine
- 70ml chicken stock
- small handful parsley, chopped
- 70g Gruyere cheese, grated
- 1 tbs olive oil
- 150g green beans
- prepare cauliflower mash for topping (see page 19)
- parsley for garnish

1. Mix chilli, pepper and salt in a bowl.
2. Chop the duck breasts.
3. Fry shallots, carrot and thyme in butter. Add a pinch of the chilli/pepper mix.
4. Cook for 4 min.
5. Add wine and chicken stock. Cook for a few mins.
6. Add duck meat and chopped parsley.
7. Cook for a further 2 min then set aside.
8. Prepare the cauli mash. Add extra salt if required and the rest of the pepper mix. Mix thoroughly.
9. Grease a baking tin; place the meat mixture in and top with the seasoned cauliflower mash.
10. Sprinkle cheese on top.
11. Bake in the oven for 25 min.
12. Prepare green beans: 5 min before the main dish is ready, fry the beans in olive oil adding salt and pepper, then add 1 tbs water and close the lid and steam for 2 min.
13. Serve cottage pie immediately.
14. Garnish with parsley and add green beans on the side.

Chapter 9 chicken and game birds

Pot Roasted Pheasant

Can use grouse, partridge or chicken.

 7g  10 min/1h10 min

- 1 tbs butter
- 1 tbs olive oil
- 1 pheasant
- 2 shallots, chopped
- 2 cloves garlic, chopped
- 2 carrots, chopped
- 50g streaky bacon, diced
- 100g mushrooms, chopped
- 2 sprigs thyme
- 2 bay leaves
- 30ml whisky
- 100ml red wine
- 1 tsp arrowroot mixed in 2 tbs water

1. *Melt butter and olive oil in a casserole.*
2. *Season pheasant with salt and pepper, then add to casserole and brown all over.*
3. *Add shallots, garlic, carrots, bacon and mushrooms to the casserole.*
4. *Add thyme and bay leaves.*
5. *Season with more salt and pepper, then pour in whisky and wine.*
6. *Simmer gently, covered with a lid, for 30 min.*
7. *Add arrowroot mixture and cook for further 30 min.*
8. *Serve with creamed cabbage.*

CHAPTER 10
meat

Chapter 10 meat

Steak Stir Fry

 5.5g   15 min

- 250g frying steak, cut in strips
- 3 cloves garlic, chopped
- 2 tbs olive oil
- 1 yellow bell-pepper, chopped
- 75g broccoli, chopped
- 50g courgettes, spiralised
- 2 tbs soy sauce
- 2 tbs vinegar
- ½ tsp ginger, chopped
- ½ tsp chilli paste

1. *Fry beef and 2 cloves garlic in olive oil.*
2. *Brown for 3 or more min until cooked nearly to your taste.*
3. *Toss in chopped veg and spiralised courgette, cover and cook for 2 min.*
4. *Add soy, vinegar, 1 clove garlic, ginger and chilli paste.*
5. *Cook for further 2 min.*
6. *Serve immediately.*

One-Pot Beef Curry with Spinach and Cauliflower

 5g   55 min

- 1 tbs coconut oil
- 1 onion, sliced,
- 2 cloves garlic, sliced
- 1 tbsp fresh ginger, sliced
- 1 tsp cumin
- 1 tsp coriander
- 1 tsp turmeric
- 1 tsp chilli
- 1 tsp ground cinnamon
- 250g steak, diced
- 150ml coconut cream
- 1 tbs ground almonds
- 150g cauliflower
- 2 handfuls spinach
- 1 handful parsley, chopped

1. *Heat coconut oil and brown onions, garlic and all spices for 2 min.*
2. *Add beef and brown; season with salt and pepper.*
3. *Add coconut cream and simmer for 30 to 40 min.*
4. *Add ground almonds.*
5. *Next, add cauli florets and cook for 3 min, then spinach on top for 1 min.*
6. *Serve immediately and garnish with parsley.*

Beef Pot Roast

SERVES 4 TO 6.

 8.5g  170°C 10 min/3h10 min

- 1 kg beef brisket
- sea salt and black pepper
- 2 tbs olive oil
- 1 onion, chopped
- 3 cloves garlic, chopped
- 125g radishes, chopped
- 125g carrots, chopped
- 3 stalks celery, chopped
- 50g mushrooms, chopped
- 1 tbs rosemary
- 1 tbs thyme
- 175ml beef stock
- 50ml red wine
- 2 tbs balsamic vinegar
- 2 tsp Dijon mustard
- bunch parsley, chopped to garnish

1. *Cover beef with salt and pepper.*
2. *Add olive oil to an ovenproof pan and brown beef all over.*
3. *Add onion and garlic and fry alongside beef.*
4. *Add radishes, carrots, celery and mushrooms to the pan*
5. *Add herbs.*
6. *Pour in the stock and red wine*
7. *Stir in balsamic and mustard.*
8. *Cook in the oven for 3 hours.*

> **TIP** *The recipes works well for oxtail. Instead of red wine,*
> *add half a bottle of dry white wine and let gently simmer for 3 hours.*
> *The meat should almost be coming off the bone.*
> *Enjoy with cauliflower rice.*

LEFT: *Oxtail browning in olive oil with onions, rosemary and thyme.*

Succulent Game Stew

Such a lovely dish – you can use any game produce.

 15g  10 min/1h40 min

- 3 tbs butter
- 1 shallot, chopped
- 2 garlic cloves, chopped
- 50g streaky bacon, diced
- 300g venison, diced
- 2 carrots, chopped
- 1 parsnip, chopped
- 1 tsp juniper berries, crushed
- 60ml red wine
- 150ml beef stock
- 1 tsp arrowroot, mixed in 3 tbs water
- 2 tsp Dijon mustard
- 2 sprigs thyme
- 2 sprigs rosemary
- 20g crème fraiche
- sea salt and black pepper

1. *Add butter to pan; fry the garlic, shallot and bacon for 2 min.*
2. *Then add the venison and brown for 2 min.*
3. *Add carrots and parsnip.*
4. *Add juniper berries, wine and stock and then arrowroot mix to thicken.*
5. *Add Dijon mustard, thyme and rosemary, and salt and pepper.*
6. *Cover the pan and cook for 90 min, stirring from time to time. If too dry, add more wine or stock.*
7. *Add crème fraiche and, if required, one tsp mustard to the sauce.*
8. *Serve immediately with Cauli Mash and Mixed Green Veg or Creamed Cabbage or Red Cabbage.*

Roast Rolled Lamb Shoulder

Simply yummy!

SERVES 4.

1g 180°C 10min/5h40 min

- 1 tbs olive oil
- 2 cloves garlic
- 1 tsp cinnamon
- 1 tsp cumin
- 1 tbs mint, chopped
- ½ red chilli, finely chopped
- ½ lemon, grated and juiced
- 600g rolled lamb shoulder

1. *To make the marinade, mix all ingredients, apart from lamb, in a bowl.*
2. *Score the lamb and rub in the marinade.*
3. *Store in the fridge for 4 hours.*
4. *Place the lamb in a roasting tin; cover and bake in the oven for 90 min.*
5. *Remove from the oven and leave to rest for 15 min.*
6. *Serve with your favourite mixed green vegetables.*

Pan-Seared Lamb Chops

2.5g 35 min

FOR MARINADE
- 4 lamb chops
- 1 clove garlic
- 2 tsp rosemary
- 2 tbs olive oil
- Salt and pepper

FOR SAUCE
- ½ shallot, diced
- 1 tbs whisky
- 1 tbs Dijon grain mustard
- 1 tsp lemon juice
- 1 tsp thyme
- butter
- 75ml cream
- 125g spinach

1. *Marinade the first 5 ingredients for 15 min.*
2. *Fry in a large frying pan with olive oil.*
3. *Cook for 4 or 5 min each side.*
4. *Remove.*
5. *Fry shallot in butter.*
6. *Add all other ingredients apart from spinach. Mix thoroughly, then whisk in cream.*
7. *Add spinach and steam for 2 min.*
8. *Re-add chops, heat through and serve.*

Lamb Vindaloo

 13g   180°C  20 min/1h

- 2 tbs ghee/butter
- ½ medium onion, sliced
- ½ bell-pepper, diced
- 2 tbs ghee/butter
- 1 clove garlic, chopped
- 300g lamb, cubed
- 300g tomatoes, chopped
- 100ml stock
- ½ lemon, juiced

SPICE MIX
- ½ tsp cardamom
- ½ tsp ground cloves
- ½ tsp ginger powder
- 1 tsp cinnamon
- ½ tsp cayenne
- ¾ tsp paprika
- 1 ½ tbsp cumin
- 1 ½ tbsp coriander

TO SERVE
- chopped coriander
- 100g plain yoghurt
- 2 tsp dried mint

1. *Add butter to a frying pan and melt over medium heat.*
2. *Add onion, bell-pepper and garlic, and sauté for 2 min.*
3. *Combine all spices in a bowl and mix with a fork.*
4. *Add diced lamb to frying pan and brown.*
5. *Add the spice mix and stir to coat the meat.*
6. *Cook for one minute.*
7. *Add chopped tomatoes, stock and lemon juice and stir.*
8. *Cover, turn heat to low and simmer for 20 min.*
9. *Combine yoghurt and mint in a separate bowl.*
10. *Remove the lid from the lamb and cook for further 20 min until the sauce is thickened and lamb tender.*
11. *Serve with cauliflower rice, fresh coriander and mint-yoghurt sauce.*

Pork Chops in Creamy Mushroom Sauce

 4g   25 min

- 3 slices bacon, chopped
- 1 tbs butter
- 2 pork chops or 4 pork medallions
- salt and pepper
- 150g mushrooms, sliced
- 2 cloves garlic, sliced
- 1 tbs olive oil
- 1 tsp thyme, chopped
- 50ml chicken stock
- 50ml cream

1. *Chop bacon and fry in butter.*
2. *Remove.*
3. *Fry chops, 4 min each side in bacon fat.*
4. *Remove.*
5. *Fry mushrooms and garlic in olive oil; add thyme.*
6. *Cook for 2 to 3 min.*
7. *Add stock and bring to boil.*
8. *Place chops back in and cook for a further few mins.*
9. *Place bacon back in.*
10. *Lower heat and add cream*
11. *Serve chops on top of the mushroom/bacon mix.*
12. *Serve with your favourite green veggies.*

Pot Roast Pork with Butternut Squash

14g 190°C 15 min/1h45 min

- 250g shoulder or loin pork
- 2 cloves garlic, sliced
- 1 small red chilli, chopped
- 2 tsp black peppercorns, ground
- 3 tbs butter
- 2 tsp thyme, chopped
- 2 bay leaves
- 2 sprigs rosemary, chopped
- 150g butternut squash, cubed
- 1 shallot, chopped
- 2 cloves garlic, sliced
- 100ml chicken stock
- 50ml white wine
- sea salt and black pepper
- 1 tsp arrowroot

FOR GLAZE

- 1 clove garlic, sliced
- 30g parmesan

1. *Cut slits in the loin and insert slivers of 1 clove garlic.*
2. *Mix the chilli and pepper and cover the pork with this mix.*
3. *Melt the butter and brown the pork on all sides.*
4. *Transfer pork to an ovenproof dish.*
5. *Add thyme, bay leaves, rosemary, butternut, 1 clove garlic and shallot surrounding the pork.*
6. *Cover and roast for 75 min.*
7. *Mix garlic and parmesan (for glaze).*
8. *Remove pork from oven and spread with glaze.*
9. *Return to oven for 15 min with the lid off to crisp up the garlic and parmesan.*
10. *Before serving, make gravy using the excess stock and a little arrowroot.*
11. *Serve with your favourite green veg.*

Pan-Fried Pork Medallions with Blackcurrant Syllabub

Blackcurrants are a rich source of vitamin C and a delicious accompaniment for pork.

 6g   35 min

- 100g blackcurrants
- 2 garlic cloves, chopped
- 3 rashers streaky bacon, chopped
- few sprigs fresh mixed herbs, chopped
- 4 pork medallions
- 150g green beans, chopped
- 1 tbs olive oil
- sea salt and black pepper

1. *Place blackcurrants in a pan with 40ml water.*
2. *Cover and cook for 10 min. The sauce should reduce with little excess water left.*
3. *Break up blackcurrants with a fork and add a pinch of salt and pepper. Set aside.*
4. *Chop garlic.*
5. *Fry garlic and bacon in a pan for 4 min. Keep tossing to ensure bacon is crispy. Take out and set aside.*
6. *Add herbs to bacon fat in the frying pan.*
7. *Cook for 15 seconds. Remove and stir into garlic/bacon mix.*
8. *Season medallions on both sides with salt and pepper.*
9. *Fry medallions for 4 or 5 min each side. When cooked, remove from the pan and let them rest. Cover with foil to retain heat.*
10. *Add salt and pepper then chopped veg to the frying pan. If not enough bacon fat left, add olive oil. Coat the veg with oil, throw in 1 or 2 tbs water.*
11. *Seal the lid and cook for 2 min.*
12. *Place medallions on a plate, cover with garlic, bacon and herb mix, and add blackcurrant sauce and veggies on the side.*
13. *Serve immediately.*

CHAPTER 11
desserts

M ost people we know love desserts. I have a friend who, when she goes out to a restaurant for dinner, always looks at the dessert menu first to determine whether she will have a starter! A bit of a dilemma for her now that she follows a low-carb diet. Changed days!

Initially, I thought it would be hard to create low-carb desserts, since desserts are so sugar dependent – which is, of course, why everyone loves them! However, nothing could be further from the truth, and our specially selected recipes are really easy to prepare.

Why not explore this section and find some that satisfy your sweet tooth without putting you over your net carb limit?

Note: One of the most popular flours used for low-carb/keto cooking is almond flour. We suggest you replace all flours with almond flour (or coconut flour if you have a nut allergy). Coconut flour is, however, second best as the consistency of coconut flour, due to its absorbency, makes it heavier and more difficult to use.

Mini Pecan Pie

This version just hits the spot and is sugar-free!

2g 175°C 10 min/30 min

- 80g pecans
- 3 tbs butter
- ½ tsp vanilla extract
- 1 egg

1. *Set aside 8 whole pecans for topping and chop the rest. Set aside.*
2. *Heat butter in pan and whisk in vanilla extract.*
3. *Remove from heat, whisk in egg and then stir in chopped pecans.*
4. *Pour mixture into 2 ramekin dishes, or one small dish, and dress with whole pecans.*
5. *Place in oven and bake for 20 min.*
6. *Serve immediately with cream or raspberry ice cream on top.*

Quick Strawberry Mousse

Ready in minutes, and quite rich!

SERVES 4

4g

10 min/20 min

- 250g double cream
- 150g strawberries, chopped
- 1 tsp vanilla extract
- ¼ tsp salt
- 2 tsp brandy
- 2 egg whites

1. *Whisk the cream until really thick.*
2. *Add strawberries, vanilla, salt and brandy.*
3. *Whisk egg whites until stiff and fold into the strawberry mix.*
4. *Chill in the fridge.*
5. *Serve in small dessert glasses.*

No-Bake Cheesecake

SERVES 8

 8g  15 mins/4h15 min

CRUST
- 250g almond flour
- ¼ tsp salt
- 3 tbs butter

FILLING
- 250g cream cheese
- 60g sour cream
- 120g double cream
- 60g coconut oil
- 1½ tsp pure vanilla extract
- 1 tsp lemon juice (double if desired)
- ½ tsp cinnamon

CRUST
1. *Mix almond flour, salt and 3 tbs melted butter.*
2. *Place in baking tin and chill in the fridge.*

FILLING
3. *Use cream cheese at room temperature and mix with sour cream, double cream, melted coconut oil, vanilla, lemon juice and cinnamon.*
4. *Place on top of cooled crust and cover with plastic wrap.*
5. *Chill in the fridge for 4 hours.*
6. *Serve with berries and cream if desired.*

Avocado Chocolate Mousse

Use chocolate in excess of 70%, preferably 100%.

Chill in the fridge for at least 1 hr so that the chocolate totally absorbs the avocado flavour.

 2.5g    15 min/1h15 min

- 50ml thick cream
- 60g of 100% dark chocolate, in pieces (create a few curls for decoration)
- 1 ripe avocado, chopped
- ½ tsp cinnamon powder
- 1 tsp vanilla extract
- ½ tsp sea salt
- few berries and chocolate curls for garnish

1. *Melt chocolate with cream in a pan.*
2. *Add all other ingredients to the pan.*
3. *Blend well – add more cream if necessary.*
4. *Place mix into 2 serving glasses and place in the fridge for 1 hour.*
5. *Garnish with chocolate curls from chocolate bar and berries.*

Pancakes with Berries and Yoghurt or Cream

 4g   10 min

- 2 eggs
- 100g cream cheese
- 2 tsp psyllium husks
- 25g coconut oil

TOPPING

- 25g raspberries
- 4 heaped tbs whipped cream

1. *Mix eggs, cream cheese, psyllium husks in a bowl.*
2. *Leave for 5 min to thicken.*
3. *Melt coconut oil in a non-stick pan.*
4. *Fry pancakes (make quite small) on med heat for 2 to 3 min on each side.*
5. *Whip cream.*
6. *Serve with raspberries and cream.*

Raspberry Ice Cream

SERVES 8

 4g

 10 min/3h10 min

- 250g raspberries
- 225g full fat cream cheese
- 375ml coconut cream
- 300g whipping cream
- 2 tsp pure vanilla extract

1. *Puree the berries, then add cream cheese and blend.*
2. *Add coconut cream and vanilla and blend again.*
3. *Whip cream separately, until stiff.*
4. *Fold the 2 separate mixtures together.*
5. *Place in container and freeze.*
6. *During the first 3 hours, stir from time to time to prevent it from getting too icy.*
7. *Remove from freezer 15 min before serving to allow time to thaw slightly.*

Blackberries and Apple Crumble

 14g   170°C   10 min/30 min

FILLING
- 1 small apple
- 60g blackberries
- 1 tsp arrowroot
- 1 tsp lemon juice
- 1 tsp cinnamon

CRUMBLE TOPPING
- 2 tbs butter, melted
- 60g almond flour
- pinch sea salt
- pinch cinnamon

8 tbs heavy cream for serving

1. *Skin and chop apple.*
2. *Place in a bowl, add blackberries, arrowroot, lemon juice and cinnamon.*
3. *Place all in an ovenproof dish.*
4. *Mix crumble ingredients and place on top of the fruit.*
5. *Bake for 20 min.*
6. *Remove from oven and allow to rest for 5 min.*
7. *Serve with cream.*

Tipsy Laird Dessert

SERVES 4

 6.5g   160°C 60 min

SPONGE

- 65g butter, melted
- 180g Mascarpone
- 2 eggs
- 1½ tsp baking powder
- Pinch sea salt

TIPSY LAIRD

- 100g berries
- 1 egg yolk
- 300g thick cream
- 1 tsp vanilla extract
- 1½ tsp almond flour
- splash or two of whisky
- 20g almonds

SPONGE

1. *Melt butter in a pan.*
2. *Blend in Mascarpone, add one egg at a time, then add melted butter and whisk.*
3. *Add baking powder and salt.*
4. *Pour mixture into a baking tin.*
5. *Bake for 20 to 25 min until golden.*
6. *Cool on rack.*

TIPSY LAIRD

7. *Divide sponge and line the bottom of 4 dessert glasses.*
8. *Add berries, pressing into the sponge to absorb the juice.*
9. *Place in the fridge.*
10. *Whisk egg yolk and set aside.*
11. *Heat 220g cream, adding vanilla extract, whisking gently.*
12. *Remove from the heat and add one ladle at a time to whisked egg yolk, mixing vigorously.*
13. *Return egg/cream mix to the pan and add the almond flour. Mix well until thickened.*
14. *Remove from heat and add whisky.*
15. *Take sponge mix from the fridge, spoon egg/cream mix on top of sponge.*
16. *Whip the remaining 80g cream and spoon on top of each glass.*
17. *Roast almonds for a few mins then gently crush them into pieces and sprinkle on top.*

CHAPTER 12
afterword

As I reflect on the contents of our book, it occurs to me that the answer was there all the time but I just didn't see it.

Let me just recap on my childhood memories of living in the glorious countryside on a hill farm in the Scottish Borders. I loved it – the countryside, the wildlife, the total freedom to run and explore everywhere and the added bonus of being surrounded by animals. It was a childhood made in heaven, and the love of the countryside has remained with me ever since. Farming was a challenging occupation then (and some find it so now as well), but it is the principles of those farming methods that stick in my mind today. Our animals were nearly all kept outside all year long and they either fed on grass and heather or were fed freshly cropped hay from that year. All this with few (if any) fertilisers used. The animals fertilised their own fields and hills.

The only fresh manure (from the dairy cows who remained indoors in the severe winters of the 1960s) used was on our extensive vegetable garden. The fruit and vegetables produced from this garden were nutritious and so, so tasty! I remember being asked to go and dig something up from the garden for lunch. You stuck your fork in, dug out the vegetable, and, lo and behold, there were worms everywhere – a gardener's dream, as this indicates highly nutritious soil. The fruit and veg were organic, long before organic became fashionable!

The animals that roamed on the hills and grassy pastures were in high demand because of their quality meat. So, the source of nutritious food was shown to me in early childhood. We ate fresh every day – with at least 2 freshly cooked meals each day. Totally different to today's world of fast food and microwave meals.

I also had the benefit of mentorship from three very strong individual women – my grandmother, whom I have often described as 'My Rock'. She was strict, but that was tempered by kindness and total encouragement (so important for a less-than-confident child), and her teaching of values remain with me to this day. The second was my mother – she was an exceptional individual: forthright, hardworking, full of forward-thinking ideas – she was definitely born before her time. And third, a very good friend of my mother who lived close by and to whom I am eternally grateful for her expert guidance and listening skills, whilst offering enormous encouragement.

I mention these ladies for two reasons: my heartfelt thanks for their guidance and support and, just as importantly, my memories of each of the three individuals showing me the benefit of eating fresh and the inherent benefits of nutritious food. When I stated before that the answer was there all the time, did I pay any attention then? Of course not! I was a tomboy who loved being out and about on the farm and had absolutely no interest in cooking at all! Luckily, I have a good memory and can now realise what these ladies were teaching me from an early age, even if I was not listening at the time!

It was only later, when health issues started to creep in, that I began looking for the answer. I discussed this with Estrelita, who was researching nutrition at the time, and together we started to reflect on how current farming methods and processed food had taken over the shelves at the supermarket. And the answer is obvious – we are what we eat.

You may wonder 'How did someone with a distinct lack of interest and flair for cooking ever write a cookbook?' It's a good question because in my twenties I did eventually learn to cook and had my fair share of disasters. One particular memory is stuffed bell-peppers. I can never look at a green pepper without thinking of that dish. The peppers were as hard as cement! I had a long way to go! I tell this story to give you hope. You may be an experienced cook or not – in either case, you will find the recipes easy to follow.

All our recipes have been prepared, tried and tested at Wellness EQ HQ.

Enjoy!

Chapter 12 afterword

Also by Estrelita van Rensburg and Issy Warrack

Eat Well or Die Slowly

Figure design:
Estrelita van Rensburg

Photography:
Francois Bothma
Estrelita van Rensburg
Issy Warrack

Cover design:
Elisabeth Heissler Design

ISBN (Paperback) 978 1 8381378 2 3

ISBN (eBook) 978 1 8381378 3 0

Visit us at www.wellnesseq.net

ACKNOWLEDGEMENTS

On the completion of our first book, *Eat Well or Die Slowly*, we realised it was a natural progression to write a low-carb cookbook. Indeed, that is what friends had already been requesting.

We sought to create an exciting cookbook with mouth-watering recipes which were simple to prepare, using, where possible, local food suppliers. In the case of meat, pasture-fed meat, for vegetables, the best of true organic from nearby farms and, for fish, quite one of the best shops anywhere! We have also been shopping at the local farmers' market where we pay close attention to the suppliers and ask searching questions to ascertain that they are the 'real deal'. We are very grateful to all our wonderful suppliers.

I (Issy) wish to thank my co-author, Estrelita, for her close collaboration on this book. She has limitless talent, having designed the content from scratch and taken the project right through to publication. For me, it was very important that this book should have the right 'feel' in terms of fresh food content and also that the knowledge of the energy you receive from eating these foods should leap at you from each page. I acknowledge the great influence of my mother, Marie Gray, who was right all along as she lovingly tended her garden using natural methods. She always said: 'The answer lies in the quality of the soil.' And she was right, whether it was in the quality of the vegetables that she grew, or the quality of the pasture on which our farm animals fed.

PHOTOGRAPH BY NADIN THOMSO

ABOUT THE AUTHORS

Growing up in two different countries, indeed two separate continents – one in Scotland and the other in South Africa – gave the authors experience of differing fresh foods. However, there is a common factor – fresh unadulterated food. Estrelita's grandparents had a farm where she spent many holidays and witnessed farm life, while Issy lived on a farm where her mother used natural farming principles as well as having a vegetable garden that sustained their food table for most of the year.

Both Issy and Estrelita had time-consuming careers and cooking fresh took a back seat for many years – actually to the detriment of their health.

They met in Scotland, having separately rekindled their interest in the principles of nutrition, and found great pleasure in discussing foods, their nutritional values, the principle of 'we are what we eat', etc. It has been a voyage of discovery: finding sources for the best nutritious fresh foods possible. Shopping from farm shops and suppliers where they can be sure of the provenance of the grass-fed meats, as well as observing the chickens roaming freely in their natural habitat.

The real fun was when they started to experiment with recipes. The kitchen became a source of great pleasure, laughter and mouth-watering tastes. And the idea for this book was born. They hope you gain as much pleasure, and health, from it as they have experienced.

Printed in Poland
by Amazon Fulfillment
Poland Sp. z o.o., Wrocław